Holy E-Mail

Second Lesson Sermons For
Advent/Christmas/Epiphany

Cycle A

Dallas A. Brauninger

CSS Publishing Company, Inc., Lima, Ohio

Copyright © 2001 by
CSS Publishing Company, Inc.
Lima, Ohio

Scripture quotations are from the *New Revised Standard Version of the Bible,* copyright
1989 by the Division of Christian Education of the National Council of the Churches of
Christ in the USA. Used by permission.

Library of Congress Cataloging-in-Publication Data

Brauninger, Dallas A., 1943-
  Holy e-mail : second lesson sermons for Advent, Christmas, and Epiphany, cycle A /
Dallas A. Brauninger.
     p. cm.
  ISBN 0-7880-1827-2 (alk. paper)
  1. Advent sermons. 2. Christmas sermons. 3. Epiphany season—Sermons. 4. Bible.
N.T. Epistles—Sermons. 5. Sermons, American—21st century. I. Title: Holy email. II.
Title.
BV4254.5 .B73 2001
252'.61—dc21   2001025105
                                                                          CIP

For more information about CSS Publishing Company resources, visit our website at
www.csspub.com.

ISBN 0-7880-1827-2   PRINTED IN U.S.A.

Dedicated to
Clarence "Clip" M. Higgins, Jr.

Table Of Contents

Introduction

Dallas Brauninger takes the reader on a spiritual journey from the beginning of Advent through the Transfiguration of our Lord by reflecting on the Epistles of Lectionary Year A. The signposts along this journey are questions or reflections one is prone to share with God. They arise out of life's journey and are shared with God via a brief e-mail.

The author is a pastor with a deep faith in Jesus Christ. She brings to vibrant life, possibly in a new perspective, the truths of the scriptures. God became more vital for me as I read each sermon.

The reader will be challenged by her sermon topics and e-mail alone. "Why, God? Enough Is Enough" illustrates the deep feeling toward God of one who has traveled through the deep valley sufferings of life. The author goes to the bedrock of faith, sharing ways God through Christ travels with us and gives us the will to live and conquer our suffering. My mind journeyed to these words of Martin Luther, "Let goods and kindred go, this mortal life also; the body they may kill; God's truth abideth still, God's kingdom is forever." With rich input Brauninger intertwines her poetry with her sermon text in the Christmas 2 sermon.

She addresses the need for more ecumenical cooperation as fewer persons today are responding to the call to pastoral ministry. "If, in time, the loss of strong denominational identities should happen, it will have a better likelihood of being a positive development fueled by compassion and the understanding of common goals," she writes.

In the last sermon of this book Brauninger aids us in exploring our understanding of God and God's role in our lives. There are challenges to keep struggling to grow in understanding of God through prayer, meditation, reading, and openness to the Spirit.

She writes, "As you and I mature in spirit, our ideas about God change. As long as we continue to grow in spirit, we will shed some former, outgrown religious beliefs. Our spiritual growth can lead to bringing discovery and depth to others."

This book offers much food for thought as you prepare sermons for Lectionary Year A. Not only will your mind be stretched but your soul will be inspired as you read. The blessing of God be with you.

Clarence M. "Clip" Higgins, Jr.

Preface

The Advent/Christmas/Epiphany epistles for Cycle A draw us toward the practical faith that this church season infuses into everyday living. Many questions from young Christian churches prompted the responses of the writers of these New Testament letters. These replies are still viable for the everyday person of this new century.

Who has not wondered: Was that you trying to get in touch with me, God? I wouldn't mind some encouragement. Will I ever figure you out, God? I could never be a saint. What is there about "Amazing Grace"? Is this only a song of universal yearning, or does your grace still matter? Do you still care about this world?

Questions are what we are all about if we are to continue to grow spiritually. So is confession. We doubt. We fear. Sometimes we need to tell someone that enough is enough. We stretch to our limit of patience. We get bored. We wonder if tenacity will prevail or if we will sink. We have moments of bliss and ponder anew the mystery of God. We wonder and grieve about the world.

We bring the everyday of our lives to worship. We lose and find our religion as God's continual epiphany of surprises reaches us. Lofty thoughts elude us most of the time. We need encouragement. We blanket earthbound disappointment with cynical attitude. We get to thinking we alone are dizzied by the switchbacks of a mountainous journey; yet we seldom let anyone else know about our silent deliberation.

A congregation is a community of questioners and confessors. Question and confession are two forms of our prayer. For many of us, these conversations with God are quick-sent prayers as brief and instant as an e-mail. Most of our prayer comes when life events raise our level of frustration, set joy to singing, or prompt puzzling about God. What if congregation and pastor were privy to

9

someone's e-mails to God, ponderings that reflect and hearten our own spiritual roaming?

This book unites sermon with prayer. It gives no absolute answers for a take-it-for-granted world. The sermons are shaped to assist hearers to connect with God and with each other and to give voice to the queries and announcements of our spiritually growing selves. These sermons aim to draw us into prayer. In each meditation, whether the imaginary e-mail writer, KDM, is putting words to our questions or speaking our confessions, the end of each e-mail message salutes God, "Lauds."

One bulletin note, chapter titles may be either the "e-mail message from KDM to God" or the "subject title," if you prefer to entice.

Did You Send That E-mail, God?

E-mail
From: KDM
To: God
Subject: Knowing When To Wake Up
Message: Did you send that e-mail, God? Lauds, KDM

I am passing on to you today the first of a series of notes transmitted by electronic mail. These notes came to the message board of a colleague early last week. Apparently they were composed by one sender, who uses the alias, KDM. Somehow, my friend got on KDM's mailing list. As best as I can tell, these notes are addressed to God. I do not know when KDM will become aware of the mix-up, so who knows how long we will be privy to this conversation.

Here is the first message: **Did you send that e-mail, God? Lauds, KDM.**

That's it — a one-liner, a query addressed to God. We have a little more to go on — a clue found in the topic box. KDM assigns the subject of this e-mail as follows: Knowing when to wake up.

Advent is about waking out of sleep to a bright star that fills the night with light. Let us take a moment this first Sunday of Advent to consider what time it is in our lives by asking three questions:

1) In what ways am I asleep to the present reality of my life?

2) In what ways am I asleep to the people around me whom I care about?

3) How am I asleep to my role in the global definition of world?

11

Advent is about moving from the gray shadows in our life into the light. Christ is that light. Advent salvation is about recognizing the movement from darkness to light, that is, God's entering our life — the life of a newly reborn individual as well as the life of the newborn in the manger.

A passage in today's scripture from the letter to the Romans catches the ear. The Apostle Paul assigns to us the responsibility of jumping out of bed. Paul, the great practical Christian, has just been telling the Roman Christians what they can do to live in God's realm. So after his long list of tips, Paul adds, "Besides this, you know what time it is, how it is now the moment for you to wake from sleep."

What intriguing words. Let us consider them, phrase by phrase:

"Besides," Paul says. Paul prods the early Christians with this word, besides. Come on, be honest with yourself, he might say today. True up. Stop the ignoring. Acknowledge what you recognize as true.

"[Y]ou know what time it is," Paul says. No one needs to tell you. You will know. No one else can tell us. We can know, however, only when we recognize that the time has come to wake up.

"[N]ow," Paul says. He speaks like a parent who wants a child to take responsibility for maturing but who also sees the necessity to point that child in the right direction. Paul gives the early Christians custody of responsibility. Then, lest they miss it, he nudges, "... [I]t is now ..."

Sometimes, we need the opinion of another person to confirm what we sense might be true. Sometimes we need an alarm clock to signal us into immediate awareness. We cannot count on raucous birds of April to wake us before dawn in late, nestless November.

Paul says, "[Besides this, you know what time it is, how it is now] *the moment."* Not some moment, not any moment, not many moments, but this one moment presents itself to us. The signs will make sense. Some event may trigger the aha of this moment. It might take form as an itch, an imperative calling, a yearning too strong to ignore. It might come as a whisper. However it comes, if we are ready, we will recognize the moment.

"Was this e-mail from you, God?" asked KDM. The source of the moment Paul speaks of is God.

"It is now the moment *for you*," Paul says, addressing the people of the Roman church in the plural form of "you." We, too, hear the message as a congregation. Then, as now, many singular "you's" comprise the collective "you." Each one of us first hears God's message as an individual. Like all of God's messages, it speaks directly to us. Then, it draws us beyond ourselves toward a wider community.

"[It is now the moment for you] *to wake from sleep*," Paul says. Sleepwalking does not count. We are not just to rise from the bed. Paul is talking fully awake here. Clear to the soul, our whole being wakes up. Wide awake and ready for action. "Besides," Paul says, "you know what time it is, how it is now the moment for you to wake from sleep."

A woman with diabetes told me how she learned in her lighter, early morning sleep to recognize a significant and potentially dangerous drop in her blood sugar level. She said a telltale nightmare would wake her. Now, according to her, this was no bland "bad dream" but a significant scare. Its signature was a terror or an unsolvable predicament. At times, it showed as a totally frustrating situation that drew her further and further into its chaos.

Despite its jolt, she said the nightmare assisted her. It roused her to sufficient consciousness to drink the fruit juice that would quick-raise her blood glucose level. At first, she said, she automatically tried a formerly reliable strategy. She would reshape the dream in her half-sleep to make it less menacing. However, even that semi-conscious effort began to pull her toward realizing her body was in trouble. She became so adept at this way of responding that she woke herself earlier and earlier in such a dream.

She began to appreciate the collaboration of her mind with her body. Her internal warning system followed this pattern: As her body approached dangerously low operating power, it must have shouted the threat to her brain. Her brain apparently invented the dream that startled her awake. Some part of her made the choice to come awake, to come out of the darkness into the light while she still could.

What strange, unexpected happenings draw us through the darkness of our lives into the light. Is this not God's promise for our welfare at work? With such magnetic power, God draws us to let go of the seductive dark.

What unusual armor God provides to enable us to wake from another sleep at the right moment. God awakens our curiosity about choosing life. Is this not also what Paul is telling us in this "wake up and pay attention" passage?

What invites us to wake up? Something from deep within us turns us around to address God. What is it that causes us even to think of God? What draws us toward God? No one knows for certain the answers to these questions. We do know that when we sense the ripe moment, it is no time to roll over. It is time to jump out of bed.

Christmas starts in Advent with the discernment that God is active. God acts in the dark, womb-like, getting-ready places. God reaches out to us to deliver us from whatever darkens our life by bringing that shadow into the light and by drawing us forward into the light.

Did you send that e-mail, God?

Welcome to Advent.

I Would Not Mind A Little Encouragement, God

E-mail
From: KDM
To: God
Subject: Embracing Hope
Message: I would not mind a little encouragement, God. Lauds, KDM

A relationship gone afoul brings a career to a halt. The death of a life partner means a move from the family home. The college of choice has already met its out-of-state quota. Failed eyesight ends driving years. Diabetic nerve damage makes emotions and clarity of thought too inconsistent to remain work effective. Arthritic fingers can no longer do repetitive computer work. Parkinson's disease forces early retirement of a plant manager. All of the people just mentioned have met the "I can't."

Our hearts, too, can resonate with the message of today's e-mail: **I would not mind a little encouragement, God. Lauds, KDM.** You and I stretch the limits when we are young, when it is fair, fun, and not a luxury. That is unlike our limits stretching us on a rack and bringing on the unholy whine. Limits tell us what we do not want to hear. Limits tell us we are finite creatures who must live within given boundaries.

I would not mind a little encouragement, God.

In early life, we discover possibility. In next decades, we acknowledge our limits. It is the human will, however, within precious seconds not measured by time that we must deal with, for

15

our bodies are cement. Limits hint that we do not measure up. Limits say we cannot compete with others despite our wanting to and despite the pull of the "ought." As we turn toward what is possible, we come to appreciate that life's nectar lies not in competition but in walking with each other along the journey.

Limits are not moral issues with dimensions of shame, worth, or self-value. Limits challenge our pride. Limits stop us. Limits hurt. Limits imprison us until, unless, we live within them.

I would not mind a little encouragement, God.

We despise what is broken about us. We apologize for it. Seeing only what is wrong in our lives, we ask God to forgive us for the brokenness within the whole.

Why not ask forgiveness, instead, when we are guilty of not respecting that we are doing the best we can?

Why not ask forgiveness when we demand of ourselves more than we are able?

Why not say, God, forgive us for not honoring what is whole amid our limits?

God, forgive us when we refuse to be thankful for the parts of our body that do work.

In adverse situations, a sense of impossibility first overrides all else. However, feeling overwhelmed by the "I can't" does not necessarily mean that we "cannot." It does not mean that we have sunk. It means that we are facing the truth of being unable to do something according to original plans. That is all it means. The temporary despair that accompanies a sense of being overwhelmed quiets as we figure out another way to do what is important to us. Limits just are.

There are two sides to impossibility. On the one hand is the "I cannot," that is, the precise detail of the inability. Sometimes in the midst of this "I cannot," our will to let go rages and nearly wins out. So strong at times is this struggle between the death wish and the will to live that we use most of our stamina just to hold on. The other side of impossibility is the "I can." The tenacity of our will to live is persistent. Most of the time we rise above the impossible intervals. We discern that defeat is only one part of limitation. Limitation also includes a sense of challenge.

I want to tell you about Fritz. He is the plant manager with Parkinson's, the paralyzing disease that causes a faulty relay between the brain and muscle. When speaking, Fritz says he has learned to wait out the silences until the words slip out. If a sentence still does not speak clearly, he accepts it. He says a matter-of-fact, "Again," and invites the sentence to repeat. Fritz has realized in the midst of the muddle of trying to communicate that hope is something he can choose. He, therefore, chooses daily to separate the disease from the person by focusing his energy on its management.

Each time Fritz designs a back-up strategy, his satisfaction overrides his frustration. The limitation that handicaps him becomes only a disability, an annoyance, a surmountable inconvenience.

Hope is something we have to choose. The "I can" shows itself as the rising energy that engenders creative and imaginative trying. When we are able to follow this drive to find another way, we move beyond mere survival and begin again to thrive.

Some times are tough to move through. Hope is something we have to choose. God is someone we have to seek. Sometimes, a single sentence is the most we can call out to God. Sometimes our best is only a few words or only a God-directed sigh. Sometimes when we need to have God near, we need more encouragement than we can summon through our own pep talks.

We would not mind a little encouragement, God.

It is not enough for us to snatch at hope like a bird flitting from limb to limb snatches at rose hips in a brier thicket. We need to embrace hope, choose hope, and grab on to hope with all our might.

Where does God come into all of this? Paul reminds us that God is God of steadfastness and of encouragement. Is not the Holy Spirit of God — from out of the somewhere or from deep within the soul — the very infusion of energy that gives us the idea, the possible solution, the urge to work around a limitation, the reach for the "I can"?

You, who no longer drive, locate a driver with a flexible schedule. You with arthritic fingers get funding for a computer adapted

17

so you can work. You with the entangled work relationship discover a career opening that fits your abilities.

You who lost a life partner and left your house find a way to surround yourself with what really matters. You, who were refused the college of your choice, begin a new search with a clearer idea of your talents. You with the diabetic fluctuations discover another profitable outlet for your creative energies and find again a fulfilling life.

All who know about the journey from hopelessness into hope recognize Emmanuel, the presence of God walking with us. All know the surprise of God's presence coming into the midst of our chaos. All of us can meet the "I can" of our lives.

Christmas happens when God's choosing hope and our choice of hope meet. Christmas happens when we remember to be curious. Christmas happens when we allow the "will to live" part of us, the part that refuses to stay stuck behind a barricade, anticipate again and figure out another way of being who God means for us to be. Christmas comes when we let God in and begin again to be practicers of thriving.

No wonder KDM signs off the e-mails with a perky, "Lauds." The final result in our relationship to God is a note of encouragement and praise.

In The Meantime, God

E-mail
From: KDM
To: God
Subject: Be Patient
Message: In the meantime, God.... Lauds, KDM

E-mail from KDM to God. Subject: Be patient. Message: **In the meantime, God.... Lauds, KDM.**
Arlo Johansen, a Great Plains agrarian, says a farmer has to think in terms of a 27-year average in order to maintain a positive work perspective. That is a long time to request patience. Farmers know the rain will come. They just do not know when it will come, if it will come in time, if it will rain too furiously or too plentifully for tender shoots, or if it will fall as hail that mangles everything in its path.
Farmers know the early rain will bring up the crop. Moisture, plus the warmth of the season, will soften the shell of the kernel so the life within it can burst forth. Later rains will carry moisture and nourishment to the seedling. They will help to sustain the crop. The last rains of the season to fall will provide a head start on the next growing season. Arlo Johansen says he usually feels at least one sigh of relief thinly sandwiched among the waiting periods of a season.
In the meantime, he has become expert at waiting. His story, however, does not stop with the germination of the seed. He also hopes for a good stand and harvest. Attention to his current crop

requires sound stewardship. He feeds the crop then provides nourishment for a future crop in a way that will avoid spoiling the land.

The farmer's job is to get the land ready, plant the seed, and judge how long the crop can be dry without endangering it. Today's farmer can study satellite reports that analyze fertilizer and moisture needs, acre by acre. As a result, an informed farmer can choose to irrigate only when it is necessary. However, no one controls hail, heavy rain, or the wind. The farmer's job is to be patient.

It is hard, however, to be patient. Consider all the waiting involved in raising a crop. There is enough waiting in farming to worry a farmer into trouble — if worry is the attitude of choice. There is enough waiting in farming to impatient a farmer into ill health — if impatience is the chosen attitude. Whatever the attitude, waiting is hard. What can we do about it?

"Be patient ...," the writer of James says, "until the coming of the Lord. The farmer waits for the precious crop from the earth, being patient with it until it receives the early and the late rains" (5:7).

The core of this ancient farming analogy is still practical today. Like the farmer, what we all do during the waiting times is our responsibility. Like the farmer, what we do has consequences. It is observed by others. It is noticed by God.

What is your precious crop? What are you waiting for? A baby, lab test results, spring, enough time to ..., enough money to ..., completion of a degree, things to slow down, things to pick up, the right job offer, death, vacation, retirement, a driver's license, better health, reconciliation, a life partner, the completion of unfinished business, a sense of purpose?

What do you do while you wait for Christmas? Let us draft a formula for what to do in the meantime. Here are five ingredients. You probably can add more.

The first is preparation. Whenever we focus on preparation, we add active, productive time to waiting. A period of productive waiting can be as valuable as the crop itself. Farmers do not forget about their crop. They keep an eye on the land. They maintain machinery. They do Internet market and scientific research.

No one can reclaim those unused hours for such groundwork at a later time. We waste hours when we fail to understand that our time here is given. If our "in the meantime" contains planning, dreaming, refining, and hoping, then it is useful time. If we attempt to escape waiting time with mindlessness or daydream, we squander it. Once a minute is gone, it has vanished. What remains is either the outcome of preparation or the lack of it.

Now add a dollop of expectation to this recipe for patience. To greet waiting time with a sense of anticipation is like a child's waiting for the second Christmas. Knowing that Christmas will arrive energizes the wait. The anticipation of just how Christmas will come to each individual adds vigor to the wait.

Such waiting is far different from simply escaping the present either by letting dread take over or by living so far ahead in time that we miss what is happening now. Expectation stands at the cusp between anxiety and hope. When we anticipate, we wait as the life within us prepares to burst forth.

The third part of this how-to formula is to exercise our capacity to say, "Yes," to hope. One of the hardest tasks of waiting is to hang on. As unknowns, uneasiness, and uncertainty stretch our elasticity, you and I can choose "in the meantime" attitudes.

The writer of James advises us to strengthen our hearts. The author understands the unholy grumble of waiting. When patience runs thin and our sense of hope wilts, we begin to take out ill humor on the nearest person. Waiting is the time to avoid running down ourselves or exploding our tension at others. Negative waiting only makes tight times worse.

Several practices help to increase our capacity to reclaim hope. Here are a few: Return to memory. Recall other times you have chosen hope and things have worked out. Divide the weight of your wait into lighter, manageable segments. Decide how much waiting time you can handle at a particular moment — a week, a day, an hour. Then let the rest of the time take care of itself.

Practice being kind to yourself and to those around you. Take generous care of yourself with exercise, the quality and quantity of food you eat, and the amount of your sleep. Keep talking with those around you. Stay alert to early signs of beginning to lose the

21

edge on hope so you can do something about it before you sink into muck.

"Prepare," "Expect," "Say yes to hope." Let us add trust to this formula. As we come to know what helps and what works against us during a waiting time, we also come to trust what we can count on. Trust what you can trust. Remember who is in charge, what is open to change, and what is unchanging.

The final ingredient for what to do in the meantime is clarity about what we are waiting for. Waiting is most difficult in situations where we are used to doing something to make things happen. However, there is a right time for patience. Patience helps when all is not yet ready. There is also a right time for impatience. When no one is doing what needs to be done to rectify a wrong, an unfairness, or injustice — this is the right time for impatience. It helps to choose the right things to wait for.

Being patient is an art as well as a skill. Patience shapes a unique form of passivity. It engenders the capacity for calm endurance. Patience is active while seemingly immobile. Patience is a waiting that comes from understanding the wait. This silent part of waiting is quiet and sometimes solitary, but it need not be empty. When we let it be empty, then boredom, anxiety, and a host of other miscreants shove their way into our soul.

Waiting can shoulder a definite goal. It gives us blessing time to think through life direction. We can transform waiting from empty endurance to waiting for something we determine is worthwhile. We can choose to concentrate on what we know or, at least, what we trust will come — like Christmas.

In the meantime, God? In the meantime, let us remember that Christmas is a promise. The coming is near. Some things are worth waiting for. The Good News of Christmas is one of them.

Even Me, God?

E-mail
From: KDM
To: God
Subject: Grace And Peace
Message: Even me, God? Lauds, KDM

At worship, a pastor welcomes her two deaf parishioners by signing, "God loves you," and "I love you." No "Hi," or "Good morning," or even a "How are you?" First of all, before anything else, come the most important connecting words, "God loves you" and "I love you."

When church folk pass the peace in a place of worship, there is a connecting with God and with one another. Children, adults, choir members, pew sitters, and ministers give and receive the same blessing. When our eyes or ears and our voices meet with these words, "May the peace of God be with you," "And with you also," we become aware of a gentling of voices. Because it is God's peace, we cannot pass this peace on with an empty heart. We cannot pass on God's peace unless we hear it for ourselves. Far more than a casual greeting, the passing of the peace is a sign of our wanting to be at peace with all around us.

What if on the street, at the store, at work, or at school, the preface to each "Hello" were, first, an unspoken wishing well for that person, "May God's peace be with you"? What if diplomats and state officials were to begin their deliberations with these words, "May God's peace be with you," or at least with that thought?

First of all, before anything else in the letters ascribed to Paul, Paul brings this traditional greeting. It is not from the apostle alone. The greeting is from God. The greeting is from Christ. It puts all that Paul says within the context of faith. This blessing tells the whole message: Grace to you and peace from God the Father and the Lord Jesus Christ.

A favorite screen saving option of computer users is a three-dimensional, increasingly finer, growing network of PVC-like pipes that are color-coded by size. God's peace might be visualized as coming through such an intricate pipeline. God is the action that starts the configuration. In our religion, Christ who comes at Christmas is the channel God chooses for spreading the peace.

Peace is not a solitary dimension between only God and us. You and I complete this relationship. As everyday persons, we are conduits for the peace that comes from Christ and from God. Peace is part of the networking triangle of holy relationships: God, other persons, and ourselves.

First of all, however, before we can listen to the words and heart of another person during a conversation, we ourselves need the grounding of God's blessing. As year adds to year in our lives, the cumulative factors about which we are sorry or ashamed can weigh us down. Whether our list of shortcomings is stubby or lanky, we all have a list that is part of the murky area of our life. In low times, we become vulnerable to certain details on this list. We need a reminder that God wishes well for us in both low and high times.

Paul's greeting to the people of the early church includes both God's peace and God's grace. Grace and peace do go hand in hand. Our Creator's hope for us is that the peace which only God can provide will embrace and sustain us. Our Savior's hope is that we also will know grace. Our awareness of God's grace and peace empowers us to let go of the burdensome and unchangeable elements in our life. Let us hear Paul's invitation to leave behind these burdens so we can move forward within the grace and peace of God.

How remarkable it is that you and I can know the serene energy of God's peace and be sustained by it regardless of the degree of turmoil or upheaval we endure. God's peace has something to do with being as well and whole as we can be within faulty bodies. It has something to do with accepting what we cannot change.

It has something to do with focusing on the particular contribution our skills, talents, and creativity can make in the world even if that world is a small actual community. The centering of peace brings hope. It has something to do with viewing this community from within the positive attitude of expectant optimism. It has something to do with God.

Peace and grace carry challenges. When we do know peace, a host of other disquieting conditions including exhaustion, thwarted efforts, emotional or physical pain, and flawed relationships may still threaten to rush in and annul it.

God's grace, also, is hard to accept. To acknowledge God's grace means we want to or ought to change. It has something to do with a new freedom to make the possible and necessary changes that draw us toward fullness of life. However, change takes effort. Change means sticking with the determination to do our best. We decide to do things differently when we sense the new freedom of grace. We acknowledge. We begin to look at a temptation and to see alternatives rather than to ignore possibility.

The birth of Christ brings a new answer to old ways of doing things. This is the free, try again of grace of which Paul speaks. Grace invites us to trust that we can bring closer together the reality of who we are and the kind of person we would like to be.

We tend to give up on ourselves when it seems no longer as easy as it once was to be a person of integrity. One goal of God's grace is to save us from ourselves. Grace turns us from self-focus alone. Grace draws us outward toward a dance with others. It invites us to notice the rest of the world and to try to make a difference. It tells us that, whether or not we intend to make a difference, how we live does influence those around us. How we live matters to those who care about us. Why not let the dance of life be graceful?

Have you noticed how living a grace-filled life permeates one's entire being? How we walk, our gait, our demeanor — all reflect our state of grace or lack of grace? When our spirit becomes graceful, so does our body. We stand up straighter. We hold the head higher. The scowl loosens from our facial muscles and births a smile. Hesitation or faltering of step turns to the steadiness of a purposeful stride. When we live with a sense of God's grace and peace, clumsiness of spirit dissipates.

This sense of God's grace and peace draws us toward a life lived in obedience to faith. In the quiet moments of this advent of our lives, let us wait and listen. Let us expect and hope for God's grace and peace to make themselves known, to come in the person of Jesus Christ. With Christ's birth, we shall find a renewed spirit in God's grace and peace. At Christmas, all whom God has created are in the direct path of God's peace and grace.

Even me, God? Yes, KDM, even you.

Does Your Grace
Still Matter, God?

E-mail
From: KDM
To: God
Subject: God's Grace
Message: Does your grace still matter, God? Lauds, KDM

Titus 2:11 reads, "For the grace of God has appeared, bringing salvation to all." The Christmas e-mail from KDM to God asks, **Does your grace still matter, God?** Lauds, KDM. The real query may be, Do we still matter enough to God for grace to happen?

Written in the name of Paul to Titus, Paul's co-worker and trouble shooter, this letter called "Titus" was a manual to church pastors of third and fourth generation Christians. Then, as now, the church was searching for its new identity in its current world. Among the threats to the church and church leaders in Paul's day were heresy, the state, and public opinion.

Now, as then, church leaders and church members are charged to encourage studying anew, recognizing anew, and assigning anew the role of the church in a new time and the new threats of the present age. Taking such responsibility is part of Christmas.

The years 2000 plus will tell us if we still care enough about the church to keep Christ and the church from becoming obsolete. In this time and this place, does God still matter enough to us that we will help open the door for God's grace to come in?

27

Let us look at Christmas through the eyes of a journalist. The five big questions that journalists ask are WHAT, WHO, WHERE, WHEN, and WHY.

First, WHAT? What is this newsworthy event? Christmas is the event. Christmas is the appearance of God's grace. The list of synonyms for grace runs long. Among the qualities of grace that stand out at Christmas are three. Grace is the compassionate love and protection that God bestows freely upon us. Grace is a favor rendered by one who need not give it. Grace is the good will of God who has plans for us and wishes well for us.

Question two, WHO? Christ is the who of Christmas. Christ is the one whose arrival we have awaited throughout the season of Advent. Christ's birth begins the giving of his life for us. The goals of his giving are to save us from our weaknesses and failings and to help us live better lives.

God also is the who of Christmas. God is the one doing the doing. God made the choice of new creation through the birth of Christ. God is the initiator of any grace that comes our way.

You and I also are the who of Christmas. We are both God's subject and God's object of Christmas. We are the receivers of God's outpouring of grace through our creator's action that is Christmas. We are the ones who, through Christ, will learn the way to live self-controlled, honest, and God-inclusive lives. When we embrace this discipline and responsibility, we become the doers who keep alive the Christian way of being within God's grace.

Question three, WHEN? December 25. No year date, Christmas was. Christmas is. Christmas spans all time. Its truth is timeless and universal. The truth of Christmas comes whenever we are in partnership with compassionate love. Whenever this love wins out in our lives, it is grace. This is Christmas.

Christ comes whenever we are in partnership with hope. Whenever hope tries to displace despair, it is grace. This is Christmas.

Christ comes whenever we are in partnership with peace. When peace tries to prevail, it is grace. This is Christmas.

Christ comes whenever we become partners with what is just. When just ways triumph, it is grace. This is Christmas.

Christ comes whenever our innermost being allows for the possibility of Christmas. Christmas is partly awaiting and partly being. We prepare the way for Christ to come whenever we choose to spend our energy on justice rather than on doing wrong. Whenever, as we wait, we promote love instead of discord, whenever we sound the persistent voice of peace above the racket of combat, and whenever we embrace hope over resignation, we acknowledge that Christmas still matters and that we still matter enough to God for grace to happen.

Now on this day, within these walls, the wait for December 25 is over. On December 25, this year 20__, Christmas is. It also is yet to be.

Next question, WHERE? As with when, the where of Christmas holds no boundary of race, economics, geography, society, sexual designation, lefthandedness, or disability. Christmas is a door-opening, welcoming event.

Christmas finds us whether we live in mansion or tent, in single-bedroom house, cardboard box, or a blanket. Pieces of Christmas surprise us in the hospital room, through Internet discovery, during a street corner conversation, and while waiting in the grocer's express lane.

Christmas flows into a care center for elders on a dull Saturday morning as a 99-year-old woman transports her companion residents to the countryside by reading aloud William Cullen Bryant's poem, "The Prairies": "Still this great solitude is quick with life...."

As Ben Corning drives in the predawn to his school janitorial job, he sees the glow of fire in the house of a family with school children. Without hesitation, he rouses the family sleeping upstairs, encourages them to hold on, then leads them to safety.

When you or I confront pain with hope, we hear the small voice of God's hope saying, "Hold on." God calls us back to life. Christmas pours into our being.

When God saves anyone, God does it without reservation. God's action and energy focus on the one God is saving. God is intent on saving this world, God's continually new, "wherever" creation. Christmas is a wherever event because God is convinced that our world is worthy of being saved.

Question four, WHY? With characteristically beautiful prose, the New English translation of this piece of scripture phrases it this way, "The grace of God has dawned upon the world with healing for all [humankind]; and by it we are disciplined" (2:11).

This is the why of Christmas. When the reality of God's grace finally dawns on us, we find it not a threat of punishment but an instrument of healing. The grace of God has appeared. Somehow, the old-fashioned word, grace, still is not worn out. Grace still amazes, grace the favor rendered by one who need not do so.

The first why of Christmas is healing. God brings healing to the insult of what is broken, hurt, divided, and wounded. Christmas does not stop with the gift of God's grace. It is not a one-day event. Not only does it save us from — from ourselves, but it saves us for — for ourselves, for a fuller life, for a wholeness, for a particular way of living that reflects having received the grace of God.

The second purpose of Christmas is its call to us. "It teaches us to have no more to do with Godlessness or the desires of this world but to live, here and now, responsible, honorable, and God-fearing lives" (v. 11, Phillip's Translation).

Why, God?
Enough Is Enough

E-mail
From: KDM
To: God
Subject: Endurance
Message: Why, God? Enough is enough. Lauds, KDM

Why, God? Enough is enough. Lauds, KDM. Enough is enough. By the time we holler these words, words shunned by supposedly sophisticated people, life circumstances have drawn us to the precipice. By the time we ask the "Why" question, you and I have forgotten about the endurance suffering is supposed to nurture.

Whether the disheartening occasion is a turmoil of relationship, extended economic chaos, the clutter of physical affliction, or a protracted uncertainty, suffering carries us to the outer reaches of our ability to cope. It can heave us into the territory of the precarious.

We get stuck there wandering through the walled wilderness of city streets. Anger, sorrow, despair, frustration — pick one. A product of fear will be there threatening to overtake and hound us into the new year. During these times, we let ourselves become enslaved by the fear of which the Hebrews sermon speaks, "slavery by the fear of death" (2:15).

Every decline of power, health, or social capacity is a symbolic if not actual little death that brings us closer to the fact of our mortality. Fed up because, despite sturdy efforts to surmount any

31

trouble, we fear being unable to make it through the present calamity. The declaration bursts out, "Enough is enough. I have had it, God. Something has to change now."

At the close of Victor Hugo's *Les Miserables*, the aged main character, Jean Valjean, has lost his will to live. His longtime physician, finally summoned, arrives too late. Jean Valjean says to him, "I am going to die." The practicer of medicine has no science to override Valjean's words. He can do nothing to turn around the man's will but offer the art of his compassion. The doctor remains with Jean Valjean as he dies.

Another mystery as puzzling as the will to die is the will to live. Failing to thrive after six weeks in an incubator, a premature infant was sent home. The doctor counseled the parents, "She is going to die anyway, so take her and love her."

Now 58, the same person reflects, "I refused to die. I was ready to live." Speaking further about the depth of this mysterious will to live that has sustained her throughout life, she adds, "My body has always spurned the journey with one system after another breaking down."

"With equal mystery," she continues, "the energy of my soul persists in finding first one alternative way and then another to do my work as a practicer of thriving." The woman has yielded to an inner persistence. Nothing she can do will turn around her life-giving, "I will."

Suffering does strange things to us. Sometimes, as if pushing God away with its bleakness, a rebellious anger causes us to use our challenges to defy God. During such vulnerable times, we are no angels. However, even at our worst, we cannot send God away. Rather than isolating us, the challenges that life changes bring potentially draw us closer to God. The writer of Hebrews grasps this, saying, "It is clear that [Christ] did not come to help angels" (2:16). When at our worst, you and I are the ones needing help.

Hebrews reminds us that God came to earth in the form of a human being who himself endured testing. By overcoming the power of death, Christ takes the fear out of meeting change. Christ saves us for living. His life invites us to view our various life dyings as finishing a chapter, completing a cycle, making a transition, or moving along on the journey.

As a result, we can choose to concentrate on life-giving attitudes. What you and I must endure remains with us. Yet we gain the capacity to transcend it — not to deny but to move through and get beyond it. Then, we can connect in empathy with others. Part of the paradox of "enough is enough" is in forgetting ourselves while remembering just enough to stay within the reality of our limitations.

By becoming earthbound and claiming us, God shares the pressures of human life. Beyond acceptance, Christ affirms our being, praising us, as Hebrews says, right there "in the midst of the congregation" (2:12).

Christ draws us into another realm. Because of the testing and suffering he endured, our defensive attitudes can melt within us. We need not waste energy explaining our situation to God. Christ's compassionate understanding is immediate. He takes the loneliness out of our suffering.

Sometimes, church folk choose an attitude of annoyance toward the hard-of-hearing. Then we wonder why the deaf stop coming to church. Another member who attends worship less frequently may no longer drive safely or cannot see the bulletin or fears bumping into someone with a cup of coffee. Disease or medication may confuse someone else.

The church, this place that might offer sustenance of courage, then ends up strengthening isolation rather than energizing the spirit of community. We have an alternative. As we recognize the common bond of being temporarily able-bodied people, our own capacity for the life-giving beauty of compassion grows.

Beauty opens gates in our fences as winter colors bring change to the western prairie. Gold and amber color tones of dried grasses deepen above the snow as the lowering sun finds them. Here, as with a piece of well-played music or other exquisite art form, a note of loneliness hums within us. When we open ourselves to enjoy the beautiful, other feelings slip in, feelings less comfortable than serene.

Several 89-plus-year-old members of a care center writing group acknowledged such feelings while experiencing beauty. One said, "A sunset makes me feel that way. The beauty of it more than the end of the day brings a twinge of loneliness but also a certain solitude." Another said, "For me, it would be in the morning when the sun rises, seeing the blue sky."

"At the edge of the Grand Canyon," remembered a third participant. "Holding my first great-grandbaby after my husband died." "Looking down over the city of Chicago at night." "The crops." "An ice-coated maple tree in early-morning sun."

Winter colors change within our souls when we notice that God is present both in loneliness and in solitude. As part of this confession, we move closer to letting God be God. Like beauty, the experience of suffering at once can take us out of ourselves and return us to our deeper selves.

God plans for us to live as well as we can. We fall short of answers as to why, some of the time, we hold on to the will to live and then, at other times, nearly succumb to letting go. Suffering's hurt keeps us earthbound. However, an interjection of beauty into our lives relieves the moment by drawing us toward another realm. It lifts us to a higher view. It gives us a breather. It revives and fortifies us.

Why does one person's will to live sustain that person and another's is not enough? We say that a neighbor fought a valiant fight but lost the fight against a cancer or AIDS or suicide. The loss had nothing to do with not fighting hard enough. Life as a fight is an image one might choose. Indeed, the journey can become as sweaty as a physical fight. However, fight may not be the apt image for pressing on. Fighting uses energy we cannot afford to waste.

When you and I have done all we think we can, when we consider life management as mostly our doing, and when we give it our best show but fail, isolation can amplify despair. We can go only so far alone. However, when the darker side that wants to call it quits obscures the light, our lighter side is still there. Despite all sorts of brokenness, it draws us toward a sense of wholeness and oneness with God.

34

Something happens to our capacity to endure suffering when we realize the one who stands before us also stands with us. Christ at once frees and helps us. Christ draws us nearer to the active faith of renewed hope. Even when we are full of our own troubles, the truth of Christ opens our truth so we, also, might live with compassion.

Sometimes, God, I Feel Marked
By An Unknown Destiny

E-mail
From: KDM
To: God
Subject: Marked With The Seal
Message: Sometimes, God, I feel marked by an unknown destiny.
Lauds, KDM

A youth makes a naive but unwise choice that changes the rest of her life. Another's obsession with killing leads to destructive behavior and his own death. A third individual happens to be in the way of harm at the wrong time. A chronic disease becomes acute. A chance introduction results in an unpredicted career focus. A casual conversation begins a lifelong partnership.

Timeless, universal questions emerge when both injurious and beneficial life accidents happen that seem beyond our control. You, also, may have asked some of the questions that follow:

Who is in charge of my life, anyway? Have I a destiny over which I have little say? In the mind of God, is there a carefully designed plan for me? Is God's obvious action in my life the result of my wishful thinking?

Sometimes I feel distant from God. Do I miss God because I fail to pay attention? Am I inept at reading the signs of God's presence? Is God's calling to me as intense as my calling out to God?

You and I are not the only ones drawn to the mystery of how our freedom ranks in the soul of an unseen God. Paul wrote to the early Christians in Ephesus about God's role as an adoptive parent

37

who has plans for chosen children. Paul prefaced all he wrote the Ephesian Christians with words about the blessing that God gives us through Christ. Listen again to God's action in this spiritual blessing. God blesses us. God chooses us. God destines us for adoption as God's children. God redeems us. God makes plans. God gives. God marks us.

Blesses, chooses, destines, redeems, plans, gives, marks — these are the action words of an active God. What if we were to measure all that happens to us within the perspective of this faithful God, whose first thought is to wish well for us?

E-mail writer, KDM, also has pondered how God's design interfaces with human freedom. KDM's note to God this week reads as follows: **Sometimes, God, I feel marked by an unknown destiny. Lauds, KDM.**

An unknown destiny. These words declare the debate that chance happenings can set off within us. Do we know the freedom of independence, or are we captives of destiny? The "unknown" part of the phrase, unknown destiny, defends the freedom that we have to live out our lives. The word "destiny" suggests that our freedom lies within a greater plan. It is God's plan. Hear both words, *unknown* and *destiny*, sing with the surprise and suspense of epiphany.

Twice in today's reading, Paul says that God destines us. First, God has destined us for adoption as God's children through Christ. Second, he says, in Christ our lives have been destined according to God's purpose. There is nothing accidental about being destined. Consider its meaning: decreed, fated, foreordained, predetermined. To some, these words imprison. But do they? To others, they free.

Destiny speaks of a plan. Our parent God cares enough about us to have a plan for us. Whether we interpret this plan as a necessary fate or as an excuse to escape personal responsibility is, however, an individual choice.

Apparently, KDM could not wait for God's reply to today's e-mail. Attached to KDM's e-mail were seven poems. As we listen to this poetry, let us ponder if it might be an assertion of KDM's

38

freedom and, also, of our own. The closest we come to understanding the Creator may be to let the untaught images of the poetry within us point toward both God's truth and our truth. We may have difficulty speaking directly about such topics. However, we might permit a poem to suggest how closely intertwined these two truths are.

Listen in the first of KDM's poems to the metaphor of active, responsive living as God's promise:

> *Prairie Sunrise*[1]
> *Early day-birthing sun*
> *Startles wind into unsettled gusts*
> *Then, up, stands suspended —*
> *Silent, full power*
> *Surveying the possibility of a new day.*

For everything, there is a plan. A Douglas fir knows it is a Douglas fir. The goal of its seed is to sprout another Douglas fir. On the floor of the great rain forest in the state of Washington, at the base of giant trees whose high canopy blocks most of the sun, the occasional fallen tree has created an opening to the sky, a path for a straw's width of sunlight to stretch to the floor. There, a rotting, long-fallen Douglas fir becomes a nursery for finger-length seedlings. Here is the poem:

> *Old Growth Forest*
> *Tiny Douglas firs*
> *Line up along a nurse log*
> *Waiting in the forest duff*
> *For a turn to sip the sun.*

Who is in charge? The path of an absent tree, the sun ray strength, a seed's identity, the will of the smallest seedling to survive, the capacity to wait for and then to take one's turn to live?

God is convenient to blame when life accidents or wrong choices cause our greatest plans to break into smithereens, as imaged in this couplet:

Smashed Dreams
Icicles severed by sun
Slice into mute snow.

KDM's poem about someone who lives with an advanced disease reflects that, even amid the puzzles of the unknown, we can find freedom within our given boundaries:

A Lot Of Living In One Year
There's a lot of living in one year:
Loving, giving, sorrow, joy.
A comfort comes in knowing
I am now a one-year plan.
Chance might surprise that map
With sudden hope.
Yet even before I embrace this day,
An accident might waste
The angry shouts that hurl through my heart.

There's a lot of living in one year:
Peace, wonder, acceptance, calm.
A comfort comes in knowing
My basic truth remains untouched.
I am still God's holy child,
Still valid, worthy still.
A comfort comes in knowing
There's a lot of living in one year.

Within the paradox of our trying to give an either/or answer to a both/and question, we sense God's contact with us remains as constant as a persistent Nebraska wind.

Nebraska Wind
Nebraska wind sweeps the plain
Flutes past pipes
Crackles tree limbs
Until it pushes at my spirit.

Even within the paradox, we resist. We refuse either to blow away or to be pushed out of the way. Much threatens along the course to change who we are; yet we also persist. Something deep within us insists upon unfolding our reason for being. It draws us toward a seemingly given and inevitable destination. This unique, identifying part of us remains even though it tapers to a whisper:

> *Pianissimo*
> *The music of my aged*
> *Mother in her chair*
> *Becomes pianissimo.*

What do we know for certain about our destiny? Paul tells the Christians at Ephesis that God has marked us, as God's adopted children, with the seal of promise and hope. This seal gives us the trust to greet what is uncharted with the upbeat attitude of a challenge. The promise and hope of this seal transforms KDM's unknown destiny into a known destiny. KDM's closing poem carries the title, "On Course."

> *On Course*
> *A poem prays me*
> *Like an opening*
> *Inner sunset.*

---

1. The copyrights of all poems cited in this sermon are held by the author.

It's The Mystery
That Keeps Me Going, God

E-mail
From: KDM
To: God
Subject: Divine Mystery
Message: It's the mystery that keeps me going, God. Lauds, KDM

At 6 a.m., January's ground of millions of crystals sparkles. Black figures stand silhouetted and still. Huge grayed forms loom from above. Now, a break — the moon hints, stars glimmer. A bird brushes against a branch of white pine — bringing a graceful snowfall. Cutting and clear, a car track leads on. It is now far. Crunching boots and padding dog feet pound.

Stand still. No earthly sound, only heaven speaks. A street lamp rudely intrudes, yet rightly. It spreads a filmy fir bough across the road. The way turns bringing a distant plow. The conversation of the world has begun.

From time to time, a few moments of silence brush against us inviting a graceful snowfall of God's mysterious presence. It is a wordless time — not for lack of words, but not needing words. It is an interlude of settling within the soul — a time-free epiphany wherein the inexplicable understanding of our being and our union with all other being grows clear.

Epiphany, obvious at a level that transcends both word and image, offers this moment to glimpse and to know the mystery of God. When we are open to the silence or, better put, when we allow the silence to open us to ourselves, we can do little other than revel in its grace.

Such a walk at winter dawn may have spawned KDM's e-mail message for this week. It reads, **It's the mystery that keeps me going, God. Lauds, KDM.** KDM's pondering calls to mind a conversation between two poets about this same mystery that kept them going. The first poet let slip that he was not a praying person. The second poet answered with the following words:[1]

> *He says he does not pray.*
> *If praying needs pious words*
> *If heart and craft pouring into a poem*
> *If soul-filled fingers talking a piano*
> *If a mouthed profanity speaking fear*
> *If two meeting the Thou of each other*
> *If the full silence of suspended time*
> *Is not praying,*
> *Then neither do I.*

The first poet then sent to the second his book about writing poetry. Its inscription read, "For Dee in the way we pray together. Fondly, Jud, 12/89."

We all have our own way of checking in with God. For some, prayer, that is, making ourselves available to God's availability to us, comes in the driver's seat of a sports utility vehicle during 7:12 a.m. gridlock. For others, it happens in the mysterious moments between dark and dawn on a morning walk beside a woods.

It would be nice if the music in the silence were always the tender, soul-filled resolution of a Beethoven pastorale. However, sometimes its notes express the equally soul-filled chaos of a movement by Stravinsky. Then, it seems either that nothing of God is in the silence or that the presence felt is discordant.

Sometimes, when we are caught within the disgraceful side of ourselves, the silence takes on the uneasy facet of the mystery of God. Sometimes we become so edgy within the silence that we fill it with anything from perpetual motion to prattle. We avoid the silence, yet the silence finds us. We avoid God, yet God finds us. Something deep inside recognizes, perks up, and takes notice.

44

Despite how sophisticated we have become, we still wonder about hell. In some shadow of our minds, despite all the talk about the loving, accepting nature of God, we wonder. The snowy limb looms overhead with the insidious, ominous presence of a God who might become so fed up with us that anger will take over.

Then, all those words about God's wishing well for us become muffled within the anxious part of silence. Like a gabble of gossip, the noise from our stock of shortcoming, shortfall, and sin rises until it drowns out any song of hope.

That part within us that believes we do not measure up waits for, even wants, a penalty. What can we do with this foreboding, negative, and disapproving side of silence? What can we do with hell? What about the imagery the word evokes?

Your imagination may conjure up torment in the shape of an inescapable lung-freezing and wind-blasting cold. You may visualize torture as a chigger-ridden and high-humidity heat. Your idea of anguish may be unending conflict. Perhaps it is the frustration of continually being unable. Whatever magnifies the unbearable for you, it crouches down there in the guilty corner waiting for the right moment to spring.

We do our children, and ourselves, a spiritual disservice if we inflict upon them the terrifying dread of a threatened place of never-ending punishment for the wicked after death. Being accountable for our misdeeds in real time is often misery enough. The call to be responsible for our actions need not carry an extra threat. Unjust and irrational acts in our present world bring sufficient lifetime torment.

What we listen for in the silence is up to us. Do you listen for a censuring God or for an encouraging God? When God enters our silence, God opens us up to what is good about us. God reveals to us the hope of our possibility, and we begin to stand up straight in the soul.

Then a startling aspect of this epiphany revelation emerges. Epiphany enters the silence of the night with its promises, its puzzles, its knowing, and its surprises. In the midst of epiphany, we find that God also frees us to let us see what is not so good about ourselves. Then the "I can" part of us begins to tremble with uncertainty. A tiny little inner part starts to quake.

It is hard to revel long in the fertile silence of an accepting God when we know we do not measure up. Have you noticed the snowball effect? When we get stuck in our imperfections, we begin to compile a list. That list grows longer and longer. It takes on greater and greater detail until it turns into a snow boulder and chases us down the hill.

As we try to make sense out of our lives, we can stand to face only a little reality at a time. We seldom stay around long enough in this aspect of the silence to discover that God is also present here. Yet when we fail to wait, we miss hearing God say, "I know. I know all about you. I am still on your side. I am still for you and with you. I share all the silence."

The mysterious presence of the spirit of God draws us with a mixture of fear and awe. So, let us enjoy the awe-filled side of our humanness. Let us receive the gift of gracious possibility. Let us also invite study of this other silence within a snowy dawning.

In singular beauty, a few flakes of snow release from a swaying tree bough. The surprising epiphany of snow gently falls upon snow.

---

1. The dialogue of these two poems took place between the author and poet Judson Jerome.

Are You Sure, God,
That You Show No Partiality?

E-mail
From: KDM
To: God
Subject: Being Inclusive
Message: Are you sure, God, that you show no partiality? Lauds,
KDM

The haughty part of us would prefer that God be partial, that is, partial to you and to me. We want to reap the benefits of having been singled out. On the other hand, our decent side wants God to show no partiality. We do yield a little, however. It is fine for God to be impartial as long as we do not need to move over and lose our place.

The Apostle Peter had just had a dream. God showed Peter that he should call no one profane or unclean. He was still deep in thought about this when messengers from a non-Jewish high officer in the Roman army arrived. They said their leader, a religious person named Cornelius, had instruction in a dream from God to go to Peter. The emissaries asked that Peter allow the centurion to come listen to him.

It was a decisive moment for Peter. Peter reminded the emissaries that it was unlawful for Jewish folk to talk to Gentiles. However, because his own dream was still fresh, he also told them that God had pointed out in this dream that Jesus' message was not exclusively for the Jewish people. It was for all people. Christ is the savior of all. It was time to expand the reach of the message.

So when, as a result of these two dreams, Cornelius, the other Gentiles, and Peter's own people gathered, the first words out of Peter's mouth were clear, "You know the message he sent to the people of Israel, preaching peace by Jesus Christ — he is Lord of *all*" (v. 36).

Peter went further, bolstering one statement with a next. He reminded his audience that Jesus "went about doing good and healing all who were oppressed by the devil" (v. 38b).

Hearing these words, Peter's followers almost must have fallen over. Peter was there in Galilee after the resurrection when Jesus came to the eleven disciples. Jesus then commissioned them to "make disciples of *all* nations" (Matthew 28:19). At that time, Peter did not really hear those words. Anyway, he did not act on them until God came personally to him in the dream. Then Peter heard.

How long does it take for you and me to hear the word that we are to be inclusive? That God is for everyone? That all who believe in Christ, regardless of who we are, receive forgiveness through Christ? Like KDM, we look around and wonder aloud, **"Are you sure, God, that you show no partiality?"** When we, also, finally hear the message for ourselves, we do understand that God shows no partiality.

Hypocrites, pretenders, frauds, liars, and everyday saints — no partiality.

Workaholics, alcoholics, drug abusers, prescription drug addicts, lottery-aholics, and degree-aholics — no partiality.

Retirees, single parents, couples of all variety, youths, children, care center residents, and the sandwich generation — no partiality.

Wheelchair users, tripod cane users, mobility cane and dog guide users, hearing device users, scooter users, motorcyclists, minivan drivers, long distance truckers, and e-mail users — no partiality.

Let us include people from all lands, races, religious persuasions, city streets, rural areas, mansions, and condominiums.

God raises no eyebrow. God shows no partiality, favoritism, or exclusivity. "In every nation anyone who fears [God] and does what is right is acceptable to [God]" (v. 35). The family, the realm of God, is all-encompassing.

Family are people to whom we matter. From the outside, people might look at the sacrament of baptism as a rite of inclusion into an exclusive organization. Does baptism say to outsiders, "Welcome to the holy club, the in-group church?" Are the marks of holy baptism a sign of exclusivity or inclusivity?

Today is the day we remember the baptism of the adult Jesus. Baptism is a setting apart in the best sense of the word. Without isolating, baptism sets us apart for God. At baptism, we acknowledge whose we are. A parent or other chosen guardian who stands at the chancel and places an infant into the arms of the minister for baptism, christening, or dedication participates in a symbolic letting go that is a precursor of future separations.

Baptism also is an act of sharing one's child. Parents recognize that their child does not belong exclusively to them. Their child is more than the sole extension of their being. Their child has unique being. Further, the child belongs to two families — the family of nurture and the family of God.

Neither does God belong exclusively to us. At first, it may have seemed so. The human understanding of God in the Old Testament of our Bible claimed God as highly political, familial, tribal, and then national. God was the God of Abraham, Isaac, and Jacob. Those down the right line could claim God as their God.

So important was this lineage that our first New Testament view of Jesus in Matthew was from the connecting genealogy. Having established genealogical legitimacy, New Testament storytellers hoped to convince others that Christ carried the proper pedigree.

You and I do the same thing when first meeting a distant relative. We verbally trace back to the connecting family — to a common third cousin, the great-aunts who were sisters, the great-great grandfather who emigrated, the man on the slave ship. We study the face for family resemblance. We confirm connection before we affirm and welcome the relative into the wider family.

Then, there is the wonderful other connection of the chosen, adopted ones. Despite no more blood connection than that of two lifemates, the welcoming bond confirms the chosen commitment to adopt.

What are your connections? What is your background? Do you have a job? Do you have money? How do you feel about this or that issue? Do you have the right degree? These are not the questions that attend the rite of holy baptism.

To become a Christian requires no surrender of part of one's given identity but rather the taking on of a wider identity. Listen again to the first question of baptism[1]: Do you desire [yourself or your child] to be baptized into the faith and family of Jesus Christ?

Desire — Do you desire? Do you yearn? Do you hunger and long? Is it your choice, your asking, your quiet request? Is it your doing? Only after this voluntary expression follow the renounce, profess, and promise questions that fill out the design of faith.

In adult baptism, there is the inner, personal side of covenant. We make the self-promises that confess belief in Christ. We pledge to live as best we can according to the way Christ lived. We promise God, ourselves, and the surrounding witnesses to resist oppression and evil, to show love and justice, and in our unique fashion to let the way we live reflect and point to Christ.

The next promises move us beyond ourselves. These community vows promise faithfulness in church membership, celebration of Christ's presence, furthering the mission of Christ in all the world, and being part of the nurturing dimension of the church that draws others toward growth in their own faith.

Baptism may be a small thing, just a few drops of water or a splash. Yet its meaning is generous. A family remembers whose they are — the other belonging, the holy connecting to the other family, forever. Baptism is just a few drops of water for you in there in your soul for the lifting up of memories as the mystery replays. So lift up this miracle of God's creation with just a few drops of water in the middle of doubting you can do a good enough job. Just a few drops of water, just a moment and a pause, as you remember the promise of God's quiet presence in just a few drops of water bringing the holy into the now. A few drops of water here in the middle of things that awake, create, and offer holy encouragement, a piece of affirmation with just a few drops of water.

---

1. Wording of the baptismal questions is from the United Church of Christ tradition.

I Could Never
Be A Saint, God

E-mail
From: KDM
To: God
Subject: Enriched
Message: I could never be a saint, God. Lauds, KDM

The e-mail chats KDM has with God are talks that you or I might likely have with God. Today's e-mail is no exception: **I could never be a saint, God. Lauds, KDM.** The conversation might continue in the following vein: Just so you know, God, I am very human. Enriched, yes; educated, yes; goal-oriented, yes; high-minded, yes; perfect, no.

You and I hesitate to claim the saintly part of ourselves. Such an acknowledgement would require us to live on a different plane. We see being saintly as an extreme — as thinking of others before ourselves, a self-denying and sacrificial attitude. Saints, we imagine, possess an essential goodness and humility that result in the quiet realization of equality, justice, and well-being for humankind.

No, we would add, there is little room for sainthood in present-day living. What is essential is my goal to carve out some space for myself. It is I who needs to survive. Only the independently wealthy can afford to be saintly. What is imperative is acquiring enough financial security to meet whatever future comes my way. I cannot be giving away at the same time I am accumulating. It would not come out right.

No, sainthood is not for me. Leave saintly living for the holy elect. I am far too human. But still, I feel something amiss with this competitive rush for the material. All the while, I admit to a cavity growing within my own spirit. Mostly, all I do is hurry, stew, and undermine any sense of well being that chances to slip in. Not only am I no saint, God, I also think my soul might be dying.

An acquaintance with a proclivity toward perfectionism once disclosed that when he was a child, he took to heart Jesus' words to be perfect. He said such an attitude drew him into serious trouble. He constantly had to face the reality that he was a selfish and ego-centric person. He was not Jesus. He could not attain perfection. He became aware of a huge gap between how he would like to be and how he was in everyday reality. He found himself slipping into a habit of self-condemnation. He felt little joy in his life. "Why try?" he asked.

A youth, an honor student previously engaged in many school activities, lost interest in her positive and hardy lifestyle after several classmates died by accident. She said, "Why put your soul and heart into doing your best when you may not even have a future? Why try?" she asked and slipped into alcohol.

A brother and sister of divorce who lost their sense of home in the constant shuffle both decided their best interest was to look out for themselves. Forget about everyone else. Why try?

What can we do about such attitudes? What is the antidote here? I love it when the Apostle Paul says, "I give thanks to God always for you." What if someone were to turn to you, lay a hand on your arm, and tell you, "I give thanks to God always for you"? Some among us would offer, "Why, thank you," in return or a hurried, "I give thanks to God for you also." Many more would be apt to say (or think to ourselves), "Really? But do you always say that? You would not give God thanks for me if you knew everything about me."

Okay, enough. Let us pause a minute. Everyone turn to your neighbor in the pew, right now. Think about something you would give thanks to God about for that person. Now, with a voice that means it, address this person directly with Paul's words: "I give thanks to God always for you."

Did you feel a little silly even though you meant what you said? You who heard these words, could you help but smile and maybe feel a sense of relief — a being in the right? Did you sit taller?

If all we learn from coming to church and to church school is regret for the shortfall, our sense of hope will crumble. Our souls will dry up until they blow away like a puff of house dust.

Each of us needs to hear that someone else believes in us. Then we can stretch beyond ourselves. Each of us needs to hear that someone else recognizes what is good about us and what is unique. Then we can feel that we count in the world around us. We need to know that we are not competing in some impossible race to be the purple-ribboned saint. Then we can recognize within ourselves the aspiration to keep trying.

Sometimes, you and I are severe with ourselves. Our measure is so exacting that we do not even try. However, something important happens to us inside when we allow ourselves to consider that at least from the other side, in someone else's eyes, outside of our skin, from another's perspective, we are not all that bad.

When others see in us the evidence of God's grace, we gain courage to look for what is good about ourselves. "Now what difference does that make?" you might ask. A big difference. This shift in attitude invites us to move from reproach to affirmation. Something happens when we begin to approve of ourselves.

It is as if Paul had read ahead of time a list of all the imperfections of the young Corinthian congregation. Beneath his words, he was communicating, "But, but, however, despite this, in spite of that, *I* see the possibility that you are. I notice the little things that you do — your graciousness to another person, a small act of kindness here, a gentle word there, your persistence in meeting your commitments, your faithfulness to your promises."

All of these things still count: just our not giving up completely in the commotion of living through each day, the chaos of everyone in the family going in different directions, the cacophony of relationships, the struggle to make ends meet, the shiver dimension in our load of responsibility.

We are to love God with all our heart, all our mind, and all our soul. What we must also remember is the faithfulness of God who calls us into community. God is for us with all God's heart, all God's mind, and all God's soul. This is why, in Paul's words, God "will also strengthen you to the end" (v. 8).

Consider one definition of a saint as an individual who keeps trying to keep this God connection. Being a saint is two-sided. According to Paul, more than simple aspiration, it is also our awareness of being called by God — not demanded by God but invited or summoned. Being a saint has something to do with the connection between God's calling to us to live the best lives we can and our hearing this invitation.

When we feel abandoned no longer, we stop giving up on ourselves. Paul did not say we were to be saints in isolation. He said, "[You are] called to be saints, together with all those who in every place call on the name of our Lord Jesus Christ" (v. 2). Together, therefore, we hear the invitation to move from the loneliness of being human into the community of those who strengthen each other in our effort to be good people.

Part of Epiphany is its surprise. When we keep the God connection, we begin again to care about the people connection. As we keep the people connection, we gain a clearer sense of ourselves and the meaning of our lives. Being a saint then takes care of itself.

What On Earth Will Bring Us Together, God?

E-mail
From: KDM
To: God
Subject: In Christ's Name
Message: What on earth will bring us together, God? Lauds, KDM

> *How long must we wait, God,*
> *for people to stop fighting*
> *nations and nations*
> *buyers and sellers*
> *big ones and little ones*
> *in-laws and relatives*
> *husbands and wives*
> *sisters and brothers*
> *for me to stop fighting with me?*
> *How long must we wait, God,*
> *before we let the Christ Child come here?*[1]

What on earth will bring us together, God? Lauds, KDM.
Must it always be a tragedy — children killing children, disaster
of rushing wind, snow, or fire, or someone's war and famine? You
and I unite quickly then. We are of same mind and same purpose
then. We are at one with outrage and horror. We vow in the
moment's intensity to act, to do, and to prevent. Our goal is to
reach out to those who suffer. We mine our resources and spend
our energy. Then we grow weary. Exhausted in spirit, we sit back
doing little until the next calamity heats us.

On another level, some aspect of our nature wants us to be at odds with each other. At our worst, we sprint to speak the first challenging word. We appear to listen for a triggering twinge in another's manner that will either set off our cutthroat spirit or shrink us into distrust. Making a sport of one-upmanship seems more enticing than nurturing a spirit of friendship. In theory, you and I would get along with everyone. In reality, we look for what is different so we can dismiss another's validity. In fact, something within us wants to hate.

At first, a woman I will call Rosa Marlin was tempted to adopt such a bleak characterization of the human spirit. Dedicated to interpreting for the deaf, Rosa had accepted a mid-year contract to sign for an elementary school child. Tense about her first work day, she transposed her anxiety to the student's equally concerned parent. Working with the child would be fine, she said, but she feared the mother might hinder her efforts.

Then she remembered that she and the mom had the same goal. They both wanted to maintain the enthusiasm as well as the uninterrupted education of a little child. Working toward that common end, the interpreter and the parent were then able to respond to difficulties before they intensified.

When you and I turn ourselves around to the right direction, we come to appreciate what is different as potentially healthy variety rather than seeing it as a threat. When we pursue what we hold in common with others, we begin to reach new levels of respect — both for others and for ourselves.

As an airplane prepared to land, a parent in a nearby seat kept up a commentary to distract his toddler son. "There's our runway down there, Ben," the dad said. "No, maybe it is not ours. I don't see a control tower. It must be another airport, one for smaller planes. Here's our airport. Just look at all those runways. There's the control tower. Big airports need a control tower."

The father spoke to his son as person to person, equal to equal. The words he spoke were not as important as his contagious attitude of interest in what he saw outside the window. A natural teacher, he chose to spend this energy engaging his young son. He also taught him how to divert his attention away from the discomfort of air pressure changes. What if you and I were to approach the world as teachers who spark curiosity about a kind of learning that dispels unhelpful myths about others?

The occasional sighted person feels insulted when a visually impaired person does not recognize who spoke at first "Hello." Rather than react with a bristle, some blind people suggest to sighted folk that it helps to identify themselves when starting an in-person conversation as they would over the phone.

A deaf woman relayed that at work, people said they would call her name several times. When she did not answer, they came up to her and asked, "Why are you mad at me?"

"I am not mad," she answered. "When I am concentrating on my work, I may miss you at first."

Others took the serious expression on her face as a sign of disagreement. "I am not disagreeing," she said. "I am working hard to follow what you are saying."

What if you and I were to respond to people with an interpretive attitude rather than a defensive stance? As includers instead of excluders? What if we were to give others the benefit of the doubt?

In today's lesson, Paul's prize question is, "Has Christ been divided?" In other words, "Don't make me your hero, people." People of Paul's day were becoming confused about where their allegiance lay. People in our day become similarly divided by a variety of admirable leaders heading a variety of deserving projects, all calling for our time and our commitment — service clubs, fraternal organizations, support groups, churches, school booster clubs.

Paul wanted to make sure that early Christians understood they were not to elevate him to a position of veneration. The power of the gathered community of Christians comes from Christ, not Paul. Jesus, not Paul, was crucified. Through Christ's redemptive act on the cross, God, not Paul, forgives us and gives us the strength to take responsibility for overcoming what separates us from God, from others, and from ourselves. The subgroups of early house churches were subgroups. They were working parts of the whole church but not supreme themselves.

These days, the diminished number of clergy available to serve churches is generating a number of cooperative agreements among denominations. Years of vying to be the greatest, highest, or best denominational branch of the church did not work. Many church bodies first splintered then slivered under the pain of quarrel and misunderstanding. Having revised former discordant postures, many now focus on common ground. We are all beginning to appreciate the benefits of diversity. We are participating in a conversation of different approaches that being a church filled with all kinds of people requires.

If, in time, the loss of strong denominational identities should happen, it will have a better likelihood of being a positive development fueled by compassion and the understanding of common goals. This is far different from actions charged with the negative energy of tactics aimed at swallowing the other church. Today's denominations are moving closer to the reality of being working parts of the one, whole church of Paul's vision.

Among the world's great ethical thinkers is the eighteenth century philosopher, Immanuel Kant. Kant believed that the moral choices we make individually in our relationships with others, that is, our ethics, help to create the kind of world we live in.[2] Kant had his own version of the Golden Rule. He wanted persons to do what is good and what is right not because of some self-serving end. Simply paraphrased, Kant's interpretation says, Whatever you are about to do, ask yourself this question first: What if everyone were to do that? Consider what would happen if your action were to become a universal law. When tempted to throw trash out of your car window, first ask: What would happen if everyone did that?

Our attitudes are contagious. Good will is contagious. If you and I are to further the cause of understanding and compassion, we must choose our attitudes with care. If we choose to approach the world as a positive place, a good place, then you and I will see that children's first experiences do not have to be in defense of themselves. Rather, our children will be free to reach out first to others in greeting.

You, O God, know what on earth will bring us together. Let us begin now.

1. Copyright held by Brauninger.

2. See George F. Thomas. *Christian Ethics And Moral Philosophy* (New York: Charles Scribner's Sons, 1955).

All These Demands
Don't Make Sense, God

E-mail
From: KDM
To: God
Subject: Demands On God
Message: All these demands don't make sense, God. Lauds, KDM

"For the message about the cross is foolishness to those who are perishing, but to us who are being saved it is the power of God" (1 Corinthians 1:18). At first look, taking time to come to church on Sunday morning may appear foolishness for those who spend one or two lifetimes of work at one or two jobs in a single week. You figure that coming to church on Sunday morning uses up at least three hours you could spend resting your mind or exercising your body or doing Internet research or chilling out or otherwise sloughing the dead outer skin of the past week,

continual shedding until it dawns on you that there will be no end to this molting of stress,

that you need to replenish at the level of spirit, refreshing your soul by the God-connecting and people-connecting that can fill your soul,

so you can meet the point of emptying yourself of negative, depleting, and exhaustive stress with a refilling and sturdy source of sustenance,

so you will have something to offer Monday morning besides emptiness.

Stop. Pause. Take a breath. Be among the foolish.

"For it is written, 'I will destroy the wisdom of the wise, and the discernment of the discerning I will thwart'" (v. 19). Twice in this First Corinthians reading, Paul quotes from the prophets. This time it is from Isaiah. We wonder how the wisdom of the wise differs from the wisdom of the rest of us. How does the wisdom of the wise differ from the wisdom of the foolish? How do we know if we are listed as wise or as foolish?

We try to be as wise as possible. Then God turns us around saying God will destroy the wisdom of the wise. We are, God says, rather to be like the foolish ones. No wonder our e-mail acquaintance says to these words, **"All these demands don't make sense, God. Lauds, KDM."**

God uniquely adjusts our capacity to perceive. God has a way of turning us around. The teachings of Jesus throw us off balance. His answers to the questions of those around him surprise us with the unexpected. They jolt us. They make new demands. They invite us to look into our own way of living with new eyes.

Verse 20: *"Where is the one who is wise? Where is the scribe? Where is the debater of this age? Has not God made foolish the wisdom of the world?"* These days, we play with conventional wisdom. This sport haws more of the cynical than of what is wise. Conventional opinions, established practice, and accepted standards are not necessarily wise. What we consider usual wisdom may become mirage.

Take another look at the so-called successful people around us. Much that appears wise seems foolish. The measure of wisdom remains a puzzle as we search for wise fools among us. When are you or I the wise fool? When do we reflect foolish wisdom? Although older folk have lived through much, many have repeated their mistakes and misjudgments. The longer we live, the less we view wisdom as an automatic accompaniment of age.

The inquisitive scholar within us wants to gain knowledge. The plethora of Internet data suggests that if we are informed, we will gain wisdom. If we can just fill ourselves with enough facts, our tired-eyed web cruises might quiet. Yet still another link beckons us to still another search. If we could just switch off the computer mind, we might come to trust and gain an intuitive understanding of what is true, what is right, what is lasting, what is prudent, and what is wise in the guise of foolishness.

Verses 26-29: *"Consider your own call, brothers and sisters: not many of you were wise by human standards, not many were powerful, not many were of noble birth. But God chose what is foolish in the world to shame the wise; God chose what is weak in the world to shame the strong; God chose what is low and despised in the world, things that are not, to reduce to nothing things that are, so that no one might boast in the presence of God."* The glitter, noise, accumulation of wealth and things, advanced schooling, human standards, and all that is of pseudo-importance in our lives really do not matter if we miss the point of our being here.

You and I define ourselves by our actions. Our daily schedule reveals what we hold to be important in life. We have the charge as people who are trying to live a Christian life to look at what our day is about. We can discern what of it really does not matter. We need to listen for what of it tells of a quiet, inner wisdom. Let us ponder what speaks of foolishness in the present world until we think about its underlying importance. Let us discover what in the way we live echoes and remembers Christ's words, "Nevertheless, I came to be with you always."

From Christ's birth to the cross and beyond, God asks us to lay aside our usual methods of determining what is real, what is valid, and what is reasonable. Lay these aside and choose simple, inexplicable belief. God has decided to save those who believe. Foolishness? Wisdom.

To some, foolishness might be defined as balancing work with play or taking time for preventative or restorative self-care. Foolishness might be looking again at what honors our type of personality, seeking your unique "I am" in your career or sense of vocation. It might be weighing the work we do with the type of work that most suits or fulfills us. Foolishness might risk paycheck, seniority, or attainment of tenure for justice. It might be be-ing rather than darting around with so much political positioning.

Consider the things you worry about and those you do something about. What do you put off and what do you take care of in matters of family, commitment, and relationship? Look at what propels you into action. Consider that foolishness might demand us to start over and discover the wisdom of the fool who appears deficient in judgment or understanding.

"He is the source of your life in Christ Jesus, who became for us wisdom from God, and righteousness and sanctification and redemption, in order that, as it is written, 'Let the one who boasts, boast in the Lord' " (vv. 30, 31).

Again, Paul reminds us through the early prophets, this time Jeremiah, that if we glory in our own wisdom, it probably is not wisdom at all. Signs did not persuade. Dotting an "i" and crossing the "t" led to a barrage of empty, legalistic gestures. That sort of wisdom did not work.

So God took all the multi-syllabic, distant faith words of the head — righteousness, sanctification, redemption, and more — and God made these words live in a new creation, Christ. God made the word into the close, heart words of being, living words.

Jesus became the wisdom God is talking about so God can get through to us at the level where it matters. Jesus became the standard we look to and, joining in the foolishness, measure everything by. Finally we, too, are drawn to proclaim the power of the new story that began with Christmas and find that we, also, are no longer perishing.

God, Please Send
Some Lofty Thoughts

E-mail
From: KDM
To: God
Subject: Truly Human, Truly God's
Message: God, please send some lofty thoughts. Lauds, KDM

Surprise us, God, with something to pull us out of the January/February doldrums. Lift us to a higher level of existence than sheer boredom or loneliness that disguises itself as monotony. Give epiphany renewal to our sense of hope. **Please, God, send some lofty thoughts. Lauds, KDM.**

Lofty thoughts portray the noble effort that you and I make when we attempt to live from the rafters of an inner wisdom. They are telling when we try to glean wisdom from elsewhere. Let us look at three persons who yearned for these lofty thoughts in the midst of their universal human frailty: the Apostle Paul, advocate of God; Jonathan Edwards, Congregationalist minister during the Great Religious Revival of the mid-1700s; and a woman I will name Marcy Archer, the parent of a thirteen-year-old non-disabled son and a seven-year-old son with cerebral palsy.

First, the Apostle Paul. In the usual Pauline letter, Paul seems to puff up himself with boasting. Moving from church to church, he continually has to establish himself as credible. His Paul-centered talk boasts about how despicable his ways had been and how great (and beyond his doing) the change is in him. He presents himself as an example of someone whose life was recast from the errant Saul to Paul the apostle.

Can you hear him saying, "If I could be so transformed, you can, too"? Or, "See how powerful and exacting God is in my life. God saved me from my wicked self. God is in charge."

Today's epistle lesson carries another tone. Early in Paul's first letter to the Corinthians, he drops the boast. He announces, "And I came to you in weakness and in fear and in much trembling" (2:3). Paul may have gained more followers with those words than from his inflated attitude. If you and I are honest, here is how most of us approach new situations. Beneath the bravura, we come with weakness, fear, and much trembling. No lofty words or self-inflation in today's scripture passage. Rather than a guru-focus on Paul's wisdom, Paul wanted to minimize his role. He wanted people to consider God's wisdom, not his wisdom. Paul was the product of God's wisdom not his own. Paul: truly human, truly God's.

Second, Jonathan Edwards. It was August 17, 1723, the penning of Resolution #70. For over a year, Jonathan Edwards had been compiling a notebook of rules for living. He had scratched them on paper with as much concentrated ardor as he would preach his scholarly, passionate sermons at First Church in Northampton, Massachusetts.

Among the first 24 guidelines for self-discipline that this nineteen-year-old entered in a single sitting was the following: #6. Resolved, to live with all my might, while I do live."[1] (For your information, all of his resolutions can be found on the web in the "Jonathan Edwards On-Line" entry in the Encarta Encyclopedia.)

The young Edwards' appetite for self-improvement persisted throughout the writing of his resolutions. Resolution #25 reads: "Resolved, to examine carefully, and constantly, what that one thing in me is, which causes me in the least to doubt of the love of God; and to direct all my forces against it."[2] His final entry read: "Let there be something of benevolence in all that I speak."[3]

Jonathan Edwards' thoughts are lofty. They offer noble ideas. Edwards pledged to read these resolutions once a week for the rest of his life. Then came a gap in his personal writing. Most likely, it was a human interval most of us can identify with. We get too busy for either self-evaluation or remedy. Not until 1739 at age 35 did Jonathan Edwards again pick up the personal pen of his youth and begin his other volume of personal writing, a diary called, "Personal Narrative."[4] (This is also available over the Internet.)

By that time, the Congregational minister had served thirteen years of a 24-year pastorate at the Northampton church. Readers of "Personal Narrative" will characterize the diary as the study of one Christian's ongoing struggle with falling short of noble thought. At midpoint in writing the seventy resolutions, Jonathan Edwards began this journal as a regular check-up of his progress with the earlier resolutions.

Early on in "Personal Narrative," he wrote, "I was a far better Christian for two or three years after my first conversion, than I am now ... I am greatly afflicted with a proud and self righteous spirit much more sensibly than I used to be formerly. I see that serpent rising and putting forth its head continually everywhere, all around me."[5]

He recalled that late in his college days — a time during which he was less diligent in monitoring his personal life — he had a severe attack of pleurisy. He became so sick that, he said, "God shook me over the pit of hell."[6]

These words offer insight into what prompted the imagery in his best known sermon, "Sinners In The Hands Of An Angry God." He preached the fiery sermon during the Great Revival in an attempt, he said, to wake up the unconverted in his congregation.

However, even the sophisticated readers in our new millennium may eventually quake at Jonathan Edwards' insistent imagery which arose from the Deuteronomy text, "Their foot shall slide in due time" (32:35). When we put ourselves into the slippery places, Edwards said, we are exposed to falling. Sooner or later, we will fall. We delude ourselves in our own schemes to avoid hell. "Only the pleasure of God," he added, "keeps wicked people at any one moment out of hell because they do deserve it."[7] Jonathan Edwards: truly human, truly God's.

Third, Marcy Archer. An ordinary yet remarkable person, Marcy Archer speaks with a quiet, resolute voice. Several prizes of lofty wisdom declare themselves as she relates the practical, day-to-day story of raising two sons, one of whom lives with severe damage from cerebral palsy.

Archer reviews the staggering contrasts between the maturation of a non-disabled son and a son with disabilities. She has schooled herself in the art of celebrating one boy's inch-by-inch sprints and the other's mile-long bursts of growing up.

"You have to find the positives and work with them," she says. "You have to have patience. You don't hide one boy at home any more than you hide him behind an attitude of pity."

"Sometimes," Archer admits, "I want to slip into giving up, but I don't. Sometimes in life, you discover you are simply in a different place than you had planned."

Reflecting on the part of being a mother who continually learns to balance the possible with the impossible, she finishes, "I try to live in the present while keeping the future in mind."

Marcy Archer: truly human, truly God's. The noble guidelines Marcy Archer chose for meeting and making her way through each day are the wise words of one with a sustaining conviction.

Here, as with Paul the apostle and with Jonathan Edwards, we sense the spirit of God having searched the spirit of Marcy Archer, the parent, in the honest journey of being human. We discern in these three persons God's underpinning of strength. It comes as a calm, deliberate, and mysterious wisdom.

God has a way of returning us to ourselves while also showing us the nobility of our spirit. In the midst of being truly human, we feel ourselves both wordlessly pulled toward reality and drawn forward to being better persons.

Could part of our being human be our capacity for openness to receive the power of God's wisdom? Despite universally human foibles, we still have a mysterious ability for the lofty thought. Beyond words anyone can give us, we find the true spirit of God as it shows us the surprising, right path that lets us — like Paul, like Jonathan Edwards, and like Marcy Archer — become turned around and found. We, also, are truly human, truly God's.

1. From THE RESOLUTIONS OF JONATHAN EDWARDS (written 1722-1723) in "Jonathan Edwards On-Line," Encarta Encyclopedia.

2. *Ibid.*

3. *Ibid.*

4. See "Jonathan Edwards On-Line" in Encarta Encyclopedia.

5. *Ibid.*

6. *Ibid.* This image is found also in Edward's sermon, "Sinners In The Hands Of An Angry God."

7. See SERMONS in "Jonathan Edwards On-Line" in Encarta Encyclopedia.

How Can I Figure You Out, God,
If My Interpretation Does Not Count?

E-mail
From: KDM
To: God
Subject: Thou
Message: How can I figure you out, God, if my interpretation does not count? Lauds, KDM

Today, we are invited to listen to a longer note from KDM. Just who is this God of yours?
My God seems to grow more limited each year.
Maybe it's time your God grew in your heart as well as in your head. Is your God only an invention, a projection of one small person? You know, of course, that God can take your questioning.
I know.
You haven't gotten rid of God, then, have you? I'll tell you, God is one tough character.
Okay, I'll tell you about my God. Sometimes my God is near. Sometimes my God is out in space. But, always, my God is.
Remember that when you have doubts about your God.
The God I believe in keeps on creating. But, does God have less influence today? Is God fading, becoming an absentee landlord? Why doesn't God do something about the messes in our world if God is so all-knowing and so all-powerful? Does God just stand there crying without tears, too?
Tell me more about this God of yours.

71

I see God in the peace-making. God and I connect with music. God lives in each germinating seed. My sense of wonder is God-sent. I know God is.

You do trust God, then.

I do.

Then, what is the source of this growing pang?

I have increasingly less to say to God. I want to say to you, God, "No more trouble, God, no more trouble." But I know things don't work that way.

Right. It is called life. Remember that you are right. I will never desert you. I can stand to hear your laments. I can take your no-words for me. I can suffer your hollering. I can endure the aching of your heart. I am as stubborn as you are. I can take it.

Okay, God.

The ways you and I communicate with God take unusual forms like the sort-of-rap, inner discussion type of God-talk we just heard. KDM says in this final e-mail to God, **How can I figure you out, God, if my interpretation does not count?**

Anyone who has set a jigsaw puzzle out on a card table respects puzzle power. As long as the puzzle remains unfinished, it lingers in an alluring front pocket of the mind. A section of color, a particular configuration of pattern, or a single elusive puzzle piece sends us away in frustration. As quickly, it lures us back.

Figuring out God is like working a jigsaw puzzle. Puzzle power keeps us coming back to address God in the midst of holy growing pangs — twinges similar to those the disciples must have known at his transfiguration. They were only beginning to understand the weight of their responsibility as Jesus' apostles. At the transfiguration, they must have wondered anew who would believe them.

And now, KDM, with all the pondering and puzzling you have brought to God, and to us, through your e-mail prayers, who says that your interpretation does not count just because it is one person's viewpoint? And who is to say that anyone's modest ideas about the Creator are invalid or sound, stupid or smart? Honest queries are valid wonderings. They yield candid conclusions because we sense the freedom in the first place to be our inquisitive selves.

The life of Jesus happened so long ago, God, we say. You and I were not there, so we have to take someone else's word. If only we could have been eyewitnesses to the power of God's transforming majesty when God gave Jesus the go-ahead.

Like Jesus, you and I are not mere stories flapping in the wind of imagination. We want to move beyond ideas of a possibly illegitimate Jesus toward the legitimate Christ to whom God says, "This is my Son, my Beloved, with whom I am well pleased" (2 Peter 1:17).

For Peter, these words confirm Jesus' authenticity from God's viewpoint. God's approval affirms all that Jesus is. We have only to take witness word. If you and I let it, Jesus' transfiguration will move us nearer to the mysterious possibility of change. This change comes into our being and causes us to be never the same again.

You and I want to make certain that our lives are at one with God's plan for us. You and I want to know that God is pleased with us. We need confirmation that God also blesses us and says, "Yes," to our very being so we might have the courage to say, "Yes," to our uniqueness — even in the midst of the questions we bark out to God in the off times. We, too, want God to confirm what we already know when we listen to the truth within us.

A neighbor couple were asked why they had not attended the family's church for so long. They said when their daughter went away to the denomination's college she took a class in religion and "lost her religion." So, they said, they too were finished with church.

Because we want God's stamp of approval when we doubt, disagree, or are skeptical, we hesitate to make our questioning known. However, where any one person is on the religious journey at a particular time is the right place for that person at that time.

Sometimes we hear ideas about God that we neither agree with nor understand. This need not indicate that our own ideas are faulty. Because the path of faith is each one's unique journey, no one else can tell us what to believe about God. We have a right to the struggle and joy of owning our own beliefs. Only then can we stretch in spirit.

As you and I mature in spirit, our ideas about God change. As long as we continue to grow in spirit, we will shed some former, outgrown religious beliefs. Our spiritual growth can lead to bringing discovery and depth to others.

No matter our age, as long as we are alive in spirit, faith and hope will thrive as issues for us. We continually encounter change, and changes set us to puzzling. Even when doubt overtakes our faith, something within us still expects a sign of hope. Even when we write God off as too distant, a piece of inner faith draws us to trust that God still hears every word, perceives all thoughts, and rejoins each sigh — so close to us is God.

How do we deal with challenging ideas? When we are not ready for them, we may miss them. If they come to us as an ill-prepared jolt, they may provoke a drastic recoil. When, however, we are ready for the invitation to grow in spirit, these same ideas stir something within us that wants to respond. A certain willingness to try on the idea overtakes us. A new spirit within us lets us loosen our hold on the old so we might expand our faith. The spirit within us lauds the leap.

We need to lose, or outgrow, our religion regularly in order to find and claim our faith. Hope is the bridge across this awkward time. The writer of Second Peter anticipates these struggles of pondering. The writer has heard the cleverly devised myths about Christ. The writer of Second Peter has wondered also what is imagined and what really happened that day on the mountain top. Second Peter wants us to know that Jesus is not mere story, not an isolated myth, but Jesus acknowledged, confirmed, and blessed by God at transfiguration.

Through the mysterious power of the Holy Spirit, God continually re-introduces us to ourselves. In essence, Second Peter encourages us to go ahead and try on our faith. When we are ready, it will fit. We can dare to hold onto the truth of empowering change until we see for ourselves when, "the day dawns and the morning star rises in [our] hearts" (1:19).

Books In This Cycle A Series

GOSPEL SET
It's News To Me! Messages Of Hope For Those Who Haven't Heard
Sermons For Advent/Christmas/Epiphany
Linda Schiphorst McCoy

Tears Of Sadness, Tears Of Gladness
Sermons For Lent/Easter
Albert G. Butzer, III

Pentecost Fire: Preaching Community In Seasons Of Change
Sermons For Sundays After Pentecost (First Third)
Schuyler Rhodes

Questions Of Faith
Sermons For Sundays After Pentecost (Middle Third)
Marilyn Saure Breckenridge

The Home Stretch: Matthew's Vision Of Servanthood In The End-Time
Sermons For Sundays After Pentecost (Last Third)
Mary Sue Dehmlow Dreier

FIRST LESSON SET
Long Time Coming!
Sermons For Advent/Christmas/Epiphany
Stephen M. Crotts

Restoring The Future
Sermons For Lent/Easter
Robert J. Elder

Formed By A Dream
Sermons For Sundays After Pentecost (First Third)
Kristin Borsgard Wee

Living On One Day's Rations
Sermons For Sundays After Pentecost (Middle Third)
Douglas B. Bailey

Let's Get Committed
Sermons For Sundays After Pentecost (Last Third)
Derl G. Keefer